T0363438

ISBN 978-0-6452329-6-7 (print)
ISBN 978-0-6452329-7-4 (digital)

The Thing About Jed

Nicola Baker

First paperback edition: 2023

Edited by: Crystal Leonardi
Cover Design by: Freya Horn, Designer in Your Pocket
Cover Photograph by: Rosana Kersh
Interior Design by: Freya Horn, Designer in Your Pocket

Bowerbird Publishing
Julatten, Queensland, Australia
www.crystalleonardi.com

The Thing About Jed

Nicola Baker

To Nicole, sitting on my shoulder every day and encouraging me to do what you couldn't.

To Ollie, you have left a mark in our lives, you will never be forgotten.

Joseph. Forever.

The life of a neurosurgeon is a wonderful blend of science, technical challenge, humanity, and, hopefully, humility. There would be few responsibilities in life as deeply meaningful as being entrusted with the care of a patient with a serious brain disease. Although every patient is important, it is not possible for any doctor to remember all their patients. But for every doctor, some patients are special; Jed Baker is special for me.

After completing neurosurgery training in Australia, I spent two years in the United States honing my skills in treating diseases of brain blood vessels. As a trainee in Australia I had been taught that there was no effective treatment for moyamoya disease, but while working at Stanford University I learned that surgery is very effective, especially if performed early in the disease process. I came back to Australia ready to take on the challenge!

I had already treated many moyamoya patients by the time I saw Jed, but he was special. Not only physically cute, he had an endearing personality that charmed the whole team. When I looked at him under anaesthetic as I prepared for his first surgery, my heart truly skipped a beat: he had a striking resemblance to my own son and I remember standing silent for a long time contemplating the reality that this disease could affect anyone.

In the many years since then, I have been privileged to remain Jed's neurosurgeon and for my relationship with Nicola and Peter to evolve into friendship. Any reader of "The Thing About Jed" will be struck by Nicola's strength and compassion. I am in awe of her energy and her ability to make a real difference. Establishing Moyamoya Australia will benefit many hundreds of patients directly, but also raise awareness of the disease amongst the medical community so that it can be diagnosed and treated more quickly.

As a teacher of the next generation of neurosurgeons, it is easy to focus on the science and technical challenges. For my own trainees, I try to also cover the humanity and humility that I believe are essential. These are difficult concepts to teach, and I have a short list of books that I encourage my trainees to read to deepen their understanding of the impacts of neurological disorders on patients and their families, and indeed the meaning of life. [1, 2, 3, 4.] "The Thing About Jed" has been added to my list, not only for these qualities, but also for an insight into the deficiencies of our current medical system and the profound impact that every single interaction with a patient and their family can have.

"The Thing About Jed" is a touching journey through the joys and sorrows of life, and will definitely leave the reader with an appreciation of the positive influence that Jed has on many people's lives. Of course, there is much more to Jed than can be revealed in a book, including that he is a genuinely talented artist!

Marcus Stoodley PhD,FRACS
Professor of Neurosurgery
Macquarie University

[1] The Diving Bell and the Butterfly - Jean-Dominique Bauby
[2] When Breath Becomes Air - Paul Kalanithi
[3] The Man Who Mistook His Wife for a Hat – Oliver Sacks
[4] The Thing About Jed – Nicola Baker

Jed was born perfect. He had all of his fingers and toes, and a little button nose. He smelled divine, he had shown all the signs of being a healthy baby boy, and Peter and I had all the dreams and hopes of new parents. We wanted to see him thrive, achieve, and be happy. We didn't realize, however, that there was an underlying issue for Jed, something insidious, silent, and deadly. What we also didn't know was that it would change the direction of our lives forever.

Today, Jed is a tallish bloke, standing at 5'9. He is taller than me but relatively average in height when standing next to his peers. He is sandy blonde, has brown eyes, and has an innocent face, primarily due to his lack of concern for the world around him. To look at him, I guess he looks 'normal.' He is toned and well-proportioned and has the physique of a powerful 19-year-old man. In terms of mates, Jed has his best friend, Taliah, but aside from the interactions that we have given him, he doesn't see a group of young people his age regularly.

To get a sense of the real Jed, you need to notice some of the things he does. He occasionally lays his head on my breast, as he has since infancy. Then he might speak, with an innocent, childlike voice, well rounded by the depth of a 19-year-old man, "I love you, mum," which may take strangers by surprise. When Jed isn't seeking comfort and starts to talk about the things that interest him, that's when we can appreciate the depth of his disability. This is when you realize that Jed is something else.

x

CONTENTS

CHAPTER 1

We're Having a Baby!

My pregnancy with Jed was your average baby-growing period. We didn't know whether we would have a boy or a girl; all Peter and I wanted was a healthy baby. We lived in a southern suburb of Cairns called Centenary Heights (now Bentley Park) and planned for Jed to be born at the Cairns Private Hospital.

On the morning of 5 October 2003, I awoke early feeling some unusual belly pains, initially mistaken for gallstone pain. I had a hot shower as the discomfort started to intensify, and once Peter began timing the contractions, we quickly realized that I was definitely in labour.

Off to the Cairns Private Hospital we went, where I negotiated pain relief options until it was too late to administer. I wonder if the midwife could sense my hatred for her at that moment. In hindsight, my erratic emotions were a subject of my intense discomfort, but I wondered if she had been trained to manage the intensity of a distressed mother-in-waiting. Of course, the hatred towards my midwife was short-lived, I promise.

And just like that, after 10 hours of my labour, Dr. Tom Wright placed Jed into my arms. I couldn't believe that this little human was something Peter and I had created, and I spent my first day as a mum marvelling at just how perfect he was. The day Jed was born was also the Football Grand Final day, so watching Peter holding his newborn son, whilst being so silently animated, was a sight to remember.

We learned all the things new parents did; that first poo is something to behold in a very cautious manner, the baby will feed when he is ready, and sleep is definitely overrated. We took videos of everyone who came to meet Jed in the hospital, which remain precious memories after many have since passed.

Jed was showered with gifts and good wishes, and then, after a few days, we were wheeled out of the hospital and sent home. We were just like any other first-time parents; we were scared, tired, elated, and had so many hopes and dreams for our son. I remember picturing a wedding ring on his little finger and dreaming about the family he might have, the work he'd do, and the stories he'd tell his children.

The first six weeks were a bit of a blur; we slept when he slept, ate when we could, changed nappies, and took many photos. I never had a hot cup of tea; it was always cold when I had time to drink it. Of course, in the first 6 weeks, we expected to give up all rights to sleep, eat hot food, or any kind of personal time, but we looked forward to Jed starting to settle into a routine and our world resolving into some kind of parenting 'normal'.

Sadly for us, the 6 weeks didn't seem to end.

CHAPTER 2

The Dreaded Sunset

Every day, as the sun went down, I was filled with a sense of dread. I knew I couldn't stop the nightfall and what was ahead of us, which was an oppressive fear. Nights felt painfully endless. There was no respite and the dark nights were the loneliest hours of our day.

Peter, Jed, and I would have dinner together, bathe and begin the evening routine of putting Jed in his cot. Despite our best efforts, however, Jed wouldn't go to sleep. On most nights, he would just cry for hours. Unlike Peter and I, Jed didn't seem to be adversely impacted by his lack of sleep. He had the face of an angel, so we continued on, loving him and persisting, sensing that this was just the way things were with a newborn baby.

On his best nights, Jed would manage only 20 minutes of sleep at a time. As parents, we quickly learned that sleep deprivation is a kind of torture. Having lived through it, I can completely empathize with anyone who has experienced the fatigue, irritability, and lack of concentration caused by sleep deprivation. Peter and I soon realized that if we were to survive this period, we would need to ensure that we both had some dedicated rest. So, we got through it by me going to bed from 7 pm to midnight, and then Peter would sleep from midnight until he had to get up for work.

We really did try everything to settle Jed. We got advice from many and tried almost every suggestion; lying on the floor next to his cot, patting him to sleep, playing gentle music, white noise, drugs, a computer or TV in his cot, we'd heard and tried it all! Friends didn't seem to understand; how could they? However, the contempt we felt from some only added to our desperation. We were told that Jed only cried because I had conditioned him to behave in that way. Others said I was comforting him too much and was behaving like a 'helicopter' parent.

During this period, I also recall feeling neurotic at times. On a particular occasion when the family had come to visit, I had decided to swing Jed gently in the hammock in an attempt to put him to sleep. Someone stirred their cup of tea with a spoon too loudly, and it was nearly enough to send me into a rage. I was furious and frustrated by their behaviour. How could they come to my home and be so inconsiderate as to stir their tea? Couldn't they see I was trying to get my baby to sleep? I also recall a little girl taking a little stuffed dog out of Jed's room and hiding it, then accusing her of lying to me when I asked her about it. Not my finest moment, but the sleep deprivation had taken the best part of me and any patience I had left.

During those early months with Jed, I was simply exhausted and didn't feel like myself. Peter was also a different man, living through it too, trying to be our protector but never really being able to protect us.

When Jed was 6 months old, I took him to a local health service to be weighed and checked. The child health care nurse was a very kind lady named Julie. She told me that I was a good mother, that Jed's inability to sleep wasn't my fault, and offered to come to my house to help me settle Jed.

I admit that I don't remember the night Julie came to our home, but Peter recalls her settling Jed to sleep and then leaving. She clearly didn't understand the depth of our struggles with our baby. Julie's early departure left us feeling abandoned before the depths of the night were even upon us. She had achieved no more or less than what we could already do ourselves and left when we needed her most. Peter and I were both well beyond our ability to function as reasonable and rational human beings. We were absolutely exhausted, plain and simple.

After another few months of battling on, I sought medical intervention of a different nature and received a referral to Riverton in Brisbane, which was a centre for teaching controlled crying to babies with sleeping issues. It was a facility run by Queensland Health and was just up the road from where I went to boarding school. I recall taking Jed for a walk in the fresh air one day during our stay and saw a local church sign saying, "if you are tired, I will give you rest". I stayed on that bench for an hour or more, looking at that sign and praying for it to be true.

On our arrival at Riverton, medical professionals checked both Jed and I, taking readings of temperature, heart rates, blood pressure, weight, and height. I was informed of their expectations and plan for our stay. Jed and I had our own room at night, but most of our time during the day was spent in a communal living area with other wired parents and babies.

During the first night, because mums are so exhausted, you are given sleeping tablets and told not to get out of bed for any reason.

You are expected to sleep while they care for your baby. During the second night, however, you are on your own, with a healthcare nurse close by. As per the instructions given to me, I recall sitting outside Jed's door while he cried. 2 minutes, 4 minutes, 6 minutes, 8 minutes, 10 minutes, and then starting again. I knew he was distressed and couldn't do anything about it, making me feel like I was punishing rather than helping him. Our days started at 5 am because sleep was not forthcoming, and I felt anxious about the next round of anguish. After 4 nights of perseverance and no improvement in Jed's sleep, we were sent home without ongoing support or recourses. More than ever, I felt like we were left in a sink-or-swim situation.

On our return home, I was so relieved to be reunited with Peter. He made me feel safe, secure and understood. My relief manifested into a flood of tears, exhaustion, and genuine sadness at our situation. I was trying to keep up my corporate lifestyle and be the happy party girl of past years, and I knew at that moment that life was substantially different from what I had anticipated it to be.

For the remainder of Jed's 1st year, we simply got on with life, and although remaining sleep-deprived and feeling helpless, we made the most of it. We felt isolated and very much alone. In our effort to remain positive, however, I decided to host a party for Jed's first birthday to draw a line in the sand, put our old life behind us, and embrace our new lives as parents, albeit tired and cranky.

I issued birthday party invitations and started planning what sort of food we would have and what presents I would get for him. I was excited for us all to reach this major milestone and have something to look forward to.

CHAPTER 3

Children can Stroke

When Jed was 11 months old, I couldn't get him to stop crying, no matter what I did. As a last resort, I prepared a nice warm shower for Jed and me, where I held him, rocked, and sang to him. 'Somewhere Over the Rainbow' was a favourite of Jed's, and water had also worked to help calm him in the past. When Jed did settle, however, I noticed something about Jed that I hadn't done before. He was twitching.

It started out very slight and only on one side of his face, but as minutes passed, it became more rhythmic and obvious. The involuntary pulses started to move down his face and into his body, going down his right arm into his hand and finally down to his foot. I watched on for a while until my parental instinct urged me to call for help.

After calling 000, I dialled my mum and told her that something wasn't right with Jed and that help was coming. I then called Peter and told him what was happening. Mum came around straight away and helplessly watched her little grandson's body continue to twitch. I remember looking up at mum standing in the driveway, watching Jed and I get into the ambulance and wondering what was going through her mind. Neither of us understood what was happening to our little blonde boy.

Before I knew it, we were being whisked into the emergency department of Cairns Hospital, where we were met by Paediatrician Dr. Tim Warnock. Little did we know that Dr. Tim would become one of our closest allies and dearly valued community members, remaining with us from this terrible day in 2004 to today.

In the emergency department, Jed was required to give blood samples. He was so little and had chubby arms, so finding a reliable vein proved challenging. Eventually, a cannula went into his arm and was strapped to a board to prevent Jed from dislodging the needle unintentionally. Hospital staff were coming and going regularly to observe Jed and administer antiseizure medication.

Up in the children's ward, we were provided a private room to wait for the pathology results and continue observations. I sat on the bed with Jed, watching him twitch, and began crying. Tears rolled down my cheeks uncontrollably as I watched my poor little boy's body suffer, despite my best efforts to love him better.

Just one of Those Things

I recall Dr. Tim telling us that they would send Jed and me to Brisbane Children's Hospital by Royal Flying Doctor Service, a service I never anticipated we would need. I am not terribly brave when it comes to small planes. It was remarkably cold once we got up into the air, and a nearby storm provided some unnerving turbulence. I must admit, however, it was quite a spectacular show from the airplane window, watching the lighting from above. I was strapped into a bed with Jed strapped onto my lap. We survived the journey, mostly because the pilot and nurse took such great care of us, but also because, during that scary adventure, I had my little boy to hold on to.

We were taken by ambulance to the Brisbane Children's Hospital emergency department on landing. I remember hearing another little baby in the cubicle beside us screaming in terror. As the curtain that was separating our cubicles was opened, I noticed that he had been cannulated through an artery in his skull. I assume because blood couldn't be drawn from his arm or foot, as was often attempted when veins were difficult to find. Occasions like these have left an indelible mark in my memories.

On the ward, we were admitted to an isolation room after being exposed to chicken pox before our arrival. Peter arrived via commercial flight shortly after Jed was admitted, and we were all exhausted.

Fortuitously, the isolation room was quite large, the size of a ward that would normally hold 6 beds and contained a therapeutic spa. Unfortunately, we were told we weren't allowed to use the spa, but the steps into it became a source of much enjoyment for Jed, climbing up and down for hours. The room also had a large window that looked down at the Brisbane Showgrounds and Lutwyche Road. We could see bright lights, trucks, trains, and everything a little boy would love to look at. We spent hours at the window looking at the magic of city life outside our hospital room.

Our early days in the hospital were spent watching on as Jed had tests, all the while fasting for MRIs and blood tests and patiently waiting for some answers.

Our Neurologist was a friendly face amoung so many. He would enter the room with his leather briefcase filled with whimsical trinkets and old-fashioned toys that he used to distract his young patients from the neurological examinations he performed on them. He was so kind to Jed, and there was something magical about how he interacted with him. Unfortunately, it wasn't enough to distract from the devastating news he delivered to us one day in our room; our 11-month-old baby had suffered a stroke.

You don't expect to hear the word stroke when speaking about your young child. Strokes, to me, were something that happened to old people, not babies.

Jed was prescribed medication to treat epilepsy, as neurology still hadn't determined what was causing his twitching. I was educated on administering Jed's injections and issued a letter that authorized me to carry syringes and paraphernalia to draw up his medication. It was a very concerning time, but we were told that "it was just one of those things, go home, and we hope never to see you again."

Due to the stroke, Jed showed significant weakness in the right side of his body; his face had drooped, his arm and hand had no strength, his walking was very skewed, and the right side of his body was 'limp.'

We returned home and got on with our lives to the best of our ability. Still sleep-deprived, we just hoped that the worst was behind us. We celebrated Jed's 1st birthday with family and friends as planned and went back to work and daycare.

A really positive experience after Jed's stroke was with one of the carers at his daycare. She put a sticker on Jed's left hand, which drove Jed to remove the sticker, encouraging him to use his stroke-effected right hand. Jed was determined, so little activities like this allowed him to recover from the stroke and repair the damage to his brain. We didn't receive any referrals for Jed's rehabilitation when he was discharged from Brisbane Children's Hospital, so little things like the stairs on the spa, stickers on his hand, and his inability to recognize his acquired brain injury (ABI) due to his young age, provided Jed with the strength he needed to recover. Strength in his body that we didn't realize was there.

Not Again…

Life continued on. Peter and I returned to work, never knowing what had caused the issues with Jed, but we regularly saw Dr. Tim in Cairns for check-ups and monitoring of Jed's condition.

One afternoon, around a year after Jed's stroke, we went for our afternoon walk with our scruffy dog and Jed in his pram, stopping at Uncles Les' house for a beer on the way home. Les and I were chatting while Jed played quietly with some rocks he'd found. I had been watching him play when I noticed his mouth doing something vaguely familiar. Could it be happening again? This time, he wasn't in distress; he was in his own little world, unintentionally blowing sweet little kisses with his mouth. The familiar rhythmic movement on Jed's face created enough concern for Peter and me to take Jed to our GP for a check-up. The next day, we were in Dr. Tim's office.

Dr. Tim was happy with what he observed in Jed on arrival, but while checking Jed's blood pressure, there was a problem that resulted in Dr. Tim recommending that we head over to the Cairns Hospital. He said his equipment didn't seem to be working correctly, so it would be good to have Jed's blood pressure checked at the hospital. Dr. Tim was very calm and confident, so we didn't feel too concerned about his recommendation. I had no idea what was coming.

On arrival at the hospital, we were ushered into a consultation room as Dr. Tim had called ahead to let the staff know to expect Jed. On checking his blood pressure, we were all alarmed to discover that Jed's blood pressure was extremely high. Evidently, Dr. Tim's equipment was working correctly, and Jed's high blood pressure resulted in being admitted to the hospital again and another trip to Brisbane Children's Hospital for further investigation.

CHAPTER 6

Children's Hospitals are Hard Places to be

Let me talk a little about being in a children's hospital. There are rules in these hospitals that are made to keep kids safe. After a bad night's sleep, the tepid showers make it impossible to have a hot, rejuvenating shower. You aren't allowed hot drinks unless you are in the parent's room, but patients aren't permitted in there. You make your roll-away bed in the evening and pack it up at the change of shift, usually around 7:00 am, so any rest you take during the day is in a chair. You aren't allowed to sleep in your child's bed for fear of asphyxiation. The only food you can access is in the hospital cafeteria, which, at the time, was deep-fried or days old. Vending machines contain chips and chocolates, but getting anything remotely healthy or light is nearly impossible. There are playrooms in the hospital for patients, where parents will invariably be approached by other parents who want to trade war stories and compare illnesses, but for the most part, they are places where an exhausted mum wants to pull a blanket over her head and hide from the world.

Having already had some experience in the Brisbane Children's Hospital, I was better prepared for the discomfort, tepid showers, and difficulties that came with having a little boy confined to his room who just wanted to play.

Soon after arriving for our second trip to Brisbane Children's Hospital, we were introduced to a Nephrologist. After substantial testing, Jed was diagnosed with stenosis of his renal arteries. Stenosis results in the narrowing of the renal artery, which affected Jed's kidney function and caused high blood pressure readings. It was also discovered that one of Jed's kidneys was the size of a shrivelled prune, and the other was not as small but was damaged nonetheless. We were devastated, to say the least. Not only did Jed have an undiagnosed issue with his brain, but he also had renal issues. It became apparent to us as parents that Jed's complicated medical issues would not be over any time soon.

Jed started on a new antiseizure medication, which introduced us to some medications' adverse impacts and side effects. Our little boy, who had barely had Panadol before his stroke, was now administered several medications to keep his blood pressure under control. We became acquainted with nuclear tests and got much practice at getting Jed to lie still. The one thing that remained extremely difficult was any interactions with needles, blood tests, and the insertion of a cannula into his tiny little arm.

Again, we were discharged from Brisbane Children's Hospital and sent home without answers.

A Name to Call This Thing

Being a patient from a rural community came with its own challenges, and the Brisbane Children's Hospital team didn't appear to sympathize with this. Jed and I were sent to Brisbane countless times for a single appointment, which required almost a full day of travel each way (we lived 2-hours' drive to our closest airport). Sadly, there didn't seem to be a holistic approach to managing Jed's condition, and this chapter of our lives went on for a year and a half.

In February 2007, on one of our regular trips to Brisbane Children's Hospital, we were invited to see some images in the doctors' rooms on the ward. My sister-in-law Janet was with us on this particular trip. The doctor opened an MRI image of Jed's brain and pointed to a grey area. I was informed that Jed had been diagnosed with Moyamoya disease. By definition, Moyamoya is a brain disease that can also be in other arteries in the body. In Jed's case, he had Moyamoya disease in his brain (causing him to stroke) and in his renal arteries (causing high blood pressure).

It was such a relief to have a name for Jed's condition, to be able to label it, and therefore be able to research and gain understanding. The most difficult part of the journey was not knowing what was causing Jed's issues for so long.

Other than the diagnosis of Moyamoya, I don't recall much else from that meeting. All I could focus on was a screaming voice inside of me that needed answers. I can remember being very calm and asking the doctor if Moyamoya would kill Jed. I was told, "no, this is not going to kill him, it's something we will watch, but it won't cause him any problems moving forward."

Very quickly after leaving the doctor's office, I googled Moyamoya disease to remain as well-informed as possible. It was a lot to take in, and it was very frightening to read that the disease is progressive, significantly affecting the mortality of people diagnosed. I had lots and lots of questions.

We were told that Moyamoya disease affects 1:1million people, so I expected that a specialist should be engaged to assist us with managing the condition, Jed's prognosis, and treatment. Yet again, however, we were packed off home with no plan, nor were we referred to a specialist.

During the years post-diagnosis with Moyamoya disease, Jed experienced Transient Ischaemic Attacks (TIA's), which behaved very similar to mild seizures. Peter and I were concerned that Jed's disease was starting to ramp up as the TIAs became more frequent. This made life very stressful for me as a mother and very stressful for us as a family. Peter and I could see something sinister taking a hold of Jed, he still wasn't sleeping, and we were all at the end of our tether.

On our regular trips to Brisbane Children's Hospital, feeling around in the dark, Jed was prescribed new medications with almost every visit. I vividly recall one trip when Jed's blood pressure had not been controlled for some time, and he continued to have TIA's. We were left in the hands of our Nephrologist's colleague, whose goal was to ensure Jed's blood pressure was controlled before he was discharged and sent home. This doctor prescribed Jed yet another medication to try but explained that it would make Jed 'hairy.' He received quite a dressing down from me at this unreasonable request; after all, Jed was only 4 years old. I was extremely frustrated after spending eighteen months travelling to Brisbane every 4 to 6 weeks. I felt that no one was proactively trying to find a permanent solution to Jed's condition and that he was being experimented on.

That particular trip ended on my birthday. We flew home and were met by a friend at our back door with a bottle of champagne. I drank that bottle without sharing it with a single soul.

CHAPTER 8

Not all Medicines are Created Equal

Before our next trip to Brisbane Children's Hospital, Peter and I had noticed that Jed was starting to suffer from nightmares, which was adding to our already difficult nights with him. This was something new, so we were concerned that, yet again, something menacing was going on with Jed's health. I've never felt more neurotic and disrespected by a team of medical practitioners than on that next trip to Brisbane Children's Hospital. All Peter and I wanted was a medical treatment plan that would allow Jed to improve and be healthy.

While Jed and I were in the hospital playroom, a social worker was sent to talk to us. She chose to ask me personal questions within earshot of other parents and children, which made me feel terribly vulnerable and completely defeated. While children buzzed past me on scooters and bikes, I was asked about how much alcohol I consumed, what home life was like for Jed and me, how my marriage was, and most shockingly, the miscarriages I suffered after Jed's birth. I felt like I was being treated like the cause of Jed's problems and wasn't shown any sympathy as the mother of a very sick little boy. My focus, however, remained on getting the best outcome for Jed, and if that meant answering these tough questions in an inappropriate setting, then I'd do it.

The hospital sent me a Pharmacist after exposing my most intimate personal details to the social worker. I was shown statistics and research on the particular medication Jed was taking, and it was evident that Jed's recent decline in health was due to an adverse drug reaction. Several alternative medications were suggested and implemented, and to much relief, Jed's symptoms began to subside.

To add to an extremely stressful trip, we also met with Jed's Nephrologist and a Vascular Surgeon from the Royal Brisbane Hospital. The surgeon recommended that Jed undergo urgent bypass surgery of his renal artery. Of course, we agreed, and while we waited the week for surgery, Jed, Peter, and I hid with our family in Brisbane. With Peter travelling to Brisbane to be with us, it was nice to have family time before Jed's first surgery. These short but significant times are what kept us all going.

CHAPTER 9

Renal Artery Bypass for a 4-year-old

The day of the dreaded surgery arrived, and after leaving Jed in the hands of the surgeon, Peter and I went to the waiting area outside the Children's Intensive Care Unit (ICU). Pacing up and down the hospital hallways when you know your child is undergoing surgery provokes feelings and emotions that are hard to articulate. Eventually, Jed was transferred to the ICU, where I waited with Peter and his sister Trish. Only one parent was allowed to enter the ICU at a time, so I went in first, feeling a strong need to get my hands on my baby boy.

I found Jed with tubes coming out of his little body everywhere. He had a cannula in his arm, a catheter collecting his urine, a massive plastic bandage across his tiny belly, and another massive bandage down the inside of his thigh. The surgeon had taken an artery from Jed's thigh and used it as the bypass material for his kidneys.

When Jed started to wake up, he became very distressed indeed. Something he also suffered from was Emergence Delirium. Putting Jed through major surgery with this condition was one of the scariest things Peter and I had ever done. Emergence Delirium results in very aggressive and confused behaviour in sufferers, particularly when woken from a general anaesthetic procedure. In the past, Jed had removed cannulas and catheters and caused bleeding to incisions. During some episodes of Emergence Delirium, Jed would kick, bite, scream, and thrash. He had bumpers on the sides of his bed, but there was really no calming him during an episode.

As he woke from surgery, expectedly, Jed kicked and screamed relentlessly. It was exhausting for him and for me, and my lack of sleep due to the stress of Jed's surgery wasn't helping. Jed was determined to fight his way out of the delirium he was trapped in.

While all of this was going on, there was an ICU nurse sitting at the end of Jed's bed, crunching down on Samboy chips. As she ate her way through the packet, the crackling sound of the chip packet was probably one of the most annoying sounds I'd ever heard in my life.

At around 3:30 am that morning, I was at my wits end, begging Jed to stop crying, asking him what he needed to stop screaming, when I heard a little voice speak to me, "Quiche," it said. I immediately sent Peter a text saying, "whatever you do, do not come into the hospital in the morning unless you have a piece of quiche with you." That was the catalyst for Jed beginning to settle, and finally, finally, this mummy also got some rest.

CHAPTER 10

Crinkly Chips

After one night in ICU, Jed was moved back to the ward and visited by Peter's sisters, who were all helping us recover from the traumatic events of the past 48 hours.

Children are incredible because they don't realize their disability or illness. If they want to do something, they will. That strength is what children use to convalesce themselves in situations of disability or injury. We had already seen this in Jed when he suffered his first stroke. Jed's attitude towards being in a hospital bed was that it wasn't part of his plan. He decided that jumping on the bed with a massive cut across his belly was his way of coping, so we stood beside the bed to ensure that he didn't fall or hurt himself.

As Jed's surgeon usually operated on adults, he had used adult dressings on Jed's incisions. When it was time to remove the dressings, it was one of those moments where we wished we had had some foresight. Children's dressings are made of paper, easily removed without causing pain to the patient, unlike the plastic, stretchy dressings used on adults, and in this case, Jed.

CHAPTER 11

The Ongoing Treadmill

In July of 2007, Jed was discharged from Brisbane Children's Hospital, returning home just in time for his fourth birthday. We had moved to a new town by this time, had made new friends, and invited everybody we knew to Jed's Pirates & Princess's birthday party. It was a magical day, full of treasure hunts, ice carvings, and fairies running through the garden. Peter, Jed, and I felt very well supported and loved by the new community and our family.

Jed's abdomen wound had healed quite well after surgery. However, he continued to have episodes of fluctuating blood pressure and TIAs. The frequent trips to Brisbane Children's Hospital didn't stop.

The week before Christmas of 2007 was very difficult. Jed spent the week in the hospital undergoing test upon test, to be sent home without answers. On Christmas Eve, we received a phone call from Brisbane Children's Hospital saying that Jed would be booked in for his second renal artery bypass surgery in early January. The Christmas period following was not one of joy, rest, and relaxation, as Peter and I nervously waited for Jed's next major surgery.

Despite our best attempts to gather more information about Jed's surgery, by mid-January, we still hadn't heard anything more from the hospital. Finally, at the end of January, we received a call from the Vascular surgeon who operated on Jed earlier in the year. His advice to me was that Jed should have been assigned a team of neurosurgeons, right from the beginning, who knew more about Moyamoya disease. Unfortunately, he believed that egos got in the way of finding the best outcome for Jed.

So, he referred us to Sydney Children's Hospital surgeon Marcus Stoodley. We were in Sydney within a matter of weeks and had two medical teams working together to schedule appointments and tests. They found us accommodation and told us where to be and when. We were sent a social worker, who was focused on how she could help us, and we were told, after years of paying hundreds of dollars for Jed's medication, that we were entitled to a health care card, greatly reducing the costs of his monthly prescriptions. Jed's medical journey was being handled very differently in Sydney, and it was a welcome change.

After many tests in Sydney, I was woken early one morning by the very tall and handsome Marcus Stoodley. Dr. Marcus advised that after reviewing Jed's results, he recommended that Jed have surgery on one side of his brain first, followed very soon after by surgery on the other half of his brain. This was the best way to keep Jed safe from another stroke.

CHAPTER 12

Don't Show Your Fear

The theatre area in Sydney Children's Hospital is rectangular, with theatre rooms separated by corridors. On the morning of Jed's first surgery with Dr. Marcus, he and I put on hospital clothing so that I could walk him all the way into the theatre. While waiting for our turn, I recall making a firm decision that if that was Jed's last day in this world, then it wouldn't be filled with fear. I did everything I could to keep him happy and laughing and not frightened of what was coming. I made jokes with him, turned gloves into animals, tickled him, and tried to help him ignore the grumbles of his fasting stomach. When Jed's name was called, I got him to climb up on my back and started to trot. After all, who doesn't love a horsey ride? We galloped all the way down the corridor, even though I had no idea where I was going. I knew that when I got there, though, Jed would be smiling.

It seemed that the sound of a child giggling was too good to resist, as many masked and gloved staff came to the theatre doors to watch our procession, a little boy laughing on the back of his mother when most children were scared and crying.

When we arrived at Dr. Marcus's theatre, we met a few other people, including the anaesthetist, and it was time for Jed to go to sleep. Jed and I noticed some large equipment on the ceiling above his bed and decided it looked like Buzz Lightyear's spaceship. As Jed took the gas mask to help him begin to relax, I looked into his brown eyes, stroking his face and his chest while I spoke to him about the adventures he would have with Buzz on the spaceship. I watched him gently slide off to sleep, knowing he was excited about the next adventure.

And then I did the worst thing that any parent could possibly do; I let go of him, turned, and walked out of the room. Once I was away from Jed, I was finally free to release the tension and emotions I had been bottling up, trying to keep Jed happy. I cried all the way back to Peter, who held me tight.

And the long day of waiting began.

CHAPTER 13

Brain Surgery Round 1

Sitting and waiting in a hospital is one of the most exhausting things you could ever do. You're waiting for news, test results, or anything that changes your situation from waiting to doing. Peter and I were extremely worried that Jed would not survive surgery and very well aware that we could be returning home this time as a childless couple.

The surgery that Jed was having involved an indirect revascularisation procedure where Dr. Marcus planned to take a blood source from an artery in front of one of Jed's ears. It would then be laid across the surface of his brain in hope that it would sense the fresh blood and use it where it was most needed, gradually feeding the damaged area of the brain. Needless to say, the brain is a pretty incredible piece of equipment. Dr. Marcus expected Jed's brain to take up to 3 months for it to completely accept the new blood source.

Many hours after Jed went into the theatre, Dr. Marcus came to tell us that the surgery went very well. Jed was being 'cleaned up' and would be transferred to ICU momentarily. Peter and I made our way to ICU, desperate to lay our hands on Jed.

When we found Jed, he had several bandages across the top of his head where burr holes had been drilled, and a long bandage down the side of his face, where the artery had been harvested. Waking a patient after neurological surgery was standard procedure in order to check for brain damage that may have occurred during surgery. It was quiet in ICU for a little while, until it was time to gently wake Jed.

The Crocodile

Emergence Delirium showed itself and continued through the afternoon and all through the night after surgery. Poor Jed was pulling lines and tubes out of his body and fighting every effort the ICU team made to keep him calm and resting. An ICU specialist gave Jed the nickname 'the crocodile' because, despite our best attempts, he was having none of it.

I felt awful watching Jed's blood pressure rise to 280 with the stress of everything happening to him. Instead of being Jed's safety, I held him down so the ICU staff could put needles back into him. Finally, at about 3:00 am Jed settled and fell asleep. Peter went to find some rest, and I did my best to sleep in the rollaway bed beside Jed.

I have a very clear memory from the early hours of that morning. At around 4:00 am, I awoke to the feeling of a weight on my leg and wondered who or what it was. My grandad Mal, who had passed when Jed was younger, appeared to me. He was sitting on the side of the bed, wearing his favourite shirt, with his hand on my leg. I asked him why he was there, and he said that he had a job to do, and that was to look after me. He stayed there until the sun saw his image disappear. His spiritual presence comforted me; it was exactly what I needed.

When Peter came into ICU the next morning, he found Jed and me in a big armchair, cuddled up to each other, asleep. Jed had a very swollen face and couldn't see out of his puffed-up eyes. His head was round from the swelling.

CHAPTER 15

Another Stroke

In the days and weeks after surgery, we stayed in Sydney and lived at Ronald McDonald House after Jed was discharged from the hospital. We were away from our family and most friends, but we were together, and we had Jed. He seemed to be doing quite well, so Peter and I decided to take him to the Royal Easter Show. We caught the bus, which in itself, was an adventure for Jed, enjoyed looking at the displays, and the animal nursery. It was a lovely time for our small family.

At around lunchtime, Jed started to get cranky which escalate quickly, despite our best efforts to comfort and settle him. We got back on the bus and took Jed to the hospital but by that time, he was in such a state of distress we decided to take him straight up to the ward, rather than go through ED. There were no beds available on the ward, so Jed was set up in the nurses' room so that his blood pressure could be monitored and we could try to settle him for the afternoon and night.

Early the next morning Jed was taken for an MRI after we were unable to settle him at all during the night. Of course, that meant another general anaesthetic for Jed and another episode of Emergence Delirium. Sitting in recovery, holding Jed, trying to keep him calm, we were met by our Neurologist, Dr. Ian. He had come to tell us that Jed had suffered another stroke. This time the damage to the brain could be seen, and Jed had lost his peripheral vision in his left eye.

Our baby boy had been stroking in front of us, and we didn't even know. Peter and I have been able to come to terms with that over the years but the sheer horror of not recognizing the signs of a stroke still astounds me.

CHAPTER 16

Brain Surgery Round 2

Jed's second round of brain surgery occurred around six weeks after the first. The day of surgery was long, as we waited for news, but the night was a lot kinder. The Sydney Children's Hospital ICU team had decided that it was better for Jed to sleep through the anticipated Emergence Delirium, so they kept him heavily sedated until morning. I appreciated this decision for both Jed's and my sake. We were moved to the ward the next day, which was a much calmer experience.

On the ward, Jed was next to a young girl who had spent most of her life in the hospital. There were only three beds on the ward, so we got to know her and her family well. When we were given the news that Jed could go home after surgery, I was so elated that I momentarily forgot where I was. Sadly, my excitement came across as rather insensitive to the family, who would likely never get to take their daughter home.

Whenever we left the hospital, our desire to get home was strong. We didn't want to see anybody or stop and buy groceries; we just wanted to get home.

The family met us at the Cairns airport on landing, and although they understood that Jed had survived two rounds of brain surgery, I don't think they realized what sort of state he would be in when he came home. He was not the happy, bouncy little boy that left to go for his surgeries. Instead, the residual damage from the surgery and the trauma his body had been through was obvious; he was awkward, unable to walk straight, and needed a lot of physical support from Peter and me. To add to the shock, Jed had several aggressive wounds across his head where holes had been drilled into his skull. I felt so sad that our loved ones saw him like that, but I realized later that it was important for them to understand the trauma we had all been through, not just Jed.

When we finally made it home to Ravenshoe, we discovered that a group of our dear friends had rallied together to decorate Jed's bedroom. They bought him a new bed, fitted it with sheets and pillows, decorated it with new curtains, and gifted Jed a child-sized driveable car. Their kindness lifted our spirits and eased our newly acquired financial stresses.

Although Jed was thrilled with his new room, he couldn't wait to jump on his trampoline. Our little boy had just had two major surgeries, but we were confident that he'd know his limits better than anyone and wouldn't jump if it didn't feel right. So, there we were, having barely walked in the door, standing around his trampoline, ready to catch him if he fell. Watching our brave little boy bounce up and down was joyous. As it turned out, the trampoline contributed substantially to Jed's recovery.

CHAPTER 17

Brain Surgery Round 3

Life became very quiet. While we were making frequent trips to Sydney, Jed's TIAs had settled, and we were getting on with life. Peter and I decided to do the same thing, and after we returned from Jed's first two rounds of surgery, we discovered that a new Baker would soon be arriving.

We were apprehensive about being pregnant again because we had already lost four babies in the stress of it all with Jed. We took one day at a time, and on 12 January 2009, less than 12 months after the worst time of our lives, Charlie Myles was born.

Charlie was a delight. He was a beautiful chubby baby, full of personality, and did everything a baby should. Charlie slept through the night early, something new for us as parents.

Jed was thrilled to have a little brother. When Charlie was born, he was crying, so Jed went to him and said, "it's okay little fella." It was the sweetest thing to see Jed so proud to have a brother to call his own.

Jed started school at Saint Teresa's primary, where he was given support for his learning difficulties and enjoyed making firm friends. To this day, he still visits the support staff at the school, who are always excited to see him.

I had started to become more willing to let the outside in. I enjoyed participating in several community events and committees, including the Chamber of Commerce, the Torimba Festival, and functions at Saint Teresa's. I felt like life had finally started moving in a positive direction.

Peter and I were also delighted to learn that another little person would join the Baker family. I was on the cusp of 40, so I was surprised to be considered advanced maternal age. I was the oldest mother in my mother's group but felt warmly welcomed and supported by my new solid city friends. They were interested in what had happened to Jed and how I had coped and were always supportive of everything we had been through as a family.

One day, around this time, I noticed something about Jed. The TIAs were back. This led to another whirlwind trip to Sydney Children's Hospital, where we were told that Jed would need bypass surgery again, but this time to the back sections of his brain, one on the left and one on the right. The good news was that the bypasses could be conducted in one operation.

Jed still suffered from Emergence Delirium, and the Sydney Children's Hospital team continued to respect the situation and left him heavily sedated after surgery. Jed's TIAs eased again after surgery and have been very few and far between since.

Jed had now received treatment for all four quarters of his brain. We knew that Moyamoya Disease was progressive, so we had long conversations with Dr. Ian about the fact that Jed had received as much intervention as possible. Sadly, this meant that Jed was, in effect, palliative. It was the first time the 'P' word had been used; we understood it but refused to let it limit how we lived our lives with Jed.

CHAPTER 18

Help Jed Meet Captain Jack

In 2014, we learned that Screen Queensland had secured filming for Pirates of the Caribbean: Dead Men Tell No Tales. During Jed's time in the hospital and throughout recovery, he had become a very passionate fan of the character from the movie franchise, Captain Jack Sparrow, played by none other than Johnny Depp.

When the news broke that there was filming for the movie scheduled in Port Douglas (a little over two hours drive from where we lived), I had to do something about it. I started a Facebook page called 'Help Jed Meet Captain Jack Sparrow,' and it went off like a rocket. It attracted much attention, including local media and many people who knew the answers to Jed's medical condition and wanted to give us all sorts of crazy solutions. The most important attention we attracted, though, was from Tracey Vieira, the CEO of Screen Queensland. I was thrilled to learn that Tracey was trying to introduce Jed to Captain Jack Sparrow in person!

Early one morning in May 2015, Tracey Vieira met the Baker family on the steps of our Gold Coast hotel. Tracey was striking, tall, blonde, and wore bright red lipstick. She oozed kindness and charm and was a delight to be around. She ushered us into a van; before we knew it, we were at Village Roadshow Studios.

We were introduced to Michael Singer, Jerry Bruckheimer's Publicist, on arrival. Michael was very complimentary, dressed in khaki and heavy-duty boots. His energy was electric, and it felt surreal to be in his presence. He and Tracey spent the day giving us the most incredible experience.

First, we met Penny Rose, an Academy Award-winning costume designer. Her room had beautiful flowing curtains, and drawings of her costumes covered the walls. There were costumes on miniature mannequins and a rack filled with garments. She had two assistants with her, and together, they created Captain Jed. The attention to detail they used on Jed's costume was outstanding, and he was proud to stride from that room as a Captain.

As we left Penny Rose's room, we met the film's leading actress, Kaya Scodelario, who travelled in true Hollywood style - on a golf buggy! Jed had a mind of his own, so instead of joining Kaya on the buggy, he marched towards a massive shed, followed by an entourage of around 20 people.

We were taken into the shed and a world of pure Disney magic; we were under the sea! It was dark, and the floor felt a little odd. My shoes were filled with minced rubber, which I later discovered was used to muffle sound. Michael warned us that we needed to be very quiet. We were taken to a row of seats with an esky filled with drinks and took in the entire experience. We sat behind a giant coral bommie and could see screens filming the action in front of the bommie. Cairns local, Brenton Thwaites, was having a sword fight with the one and only Captain Jack Sparrow, live, in the flesh!

Johnny Depp came to the back of the bommie and, in full Captain Jack character, called for 'Captain Jed.' That was the moment we met Hollywood Royalty, Johnny Depp.

Our time with Johnny was incredible. He was determined to connect with Jed and communicate with him on that level, while he flipped out of character and spent time chatting with the rest of the family. Despite being a very hot day, he remained in full costume and generously gave his time to us.

After around 45 minutes with Johnny, it was time for him to return to work. Of course, every good mother shows gratitude, so I hugged him to illustrate my appreciation. He bid us all goodbye, but his interaction with little Lucy, who was only three at the time, was pure gold. He asked her for a cuddle, and she said no. So, he asked her for a high five, but again, no. Finally, he asked her for a handshake; again, it was a no, so he picked her up and squealed that he would tickle her; it was such a beautiful interaction.

Michael and Tracey were not done with us yet; they had more exciting things for us to do! We were taken in the van to the site where the pirate ships were based, and we got to go on The Black Pearl! When I say that the ship was authentic, believe me. It was rickety; the floorboards had a definite creak in them, and let me say that the deck of a boat is a long way from the bottom of a boat!

We were invited to have lunch with the crew, and it was a complete surprise to bump into an old friend from school, who had made his life in logistics.

The entire day was a gift to us; we loved spending time with Michael and Tracey, with Johnny, and with the entire entourage that had joined us throughout the day. Penny Rose told Jed he could bring his costume home; it remains here, safe with us.

I had pre-planned to show my gratitude to Johnny in a very country way, and had baked him a Fruit cake (full of rum). I had gathered several locally produced artisan products, including a yummy bundle of fudge made by my dear friend Nicole.

I am told that Johnny ate my cake in one sitting; I was so pleased.

Jed

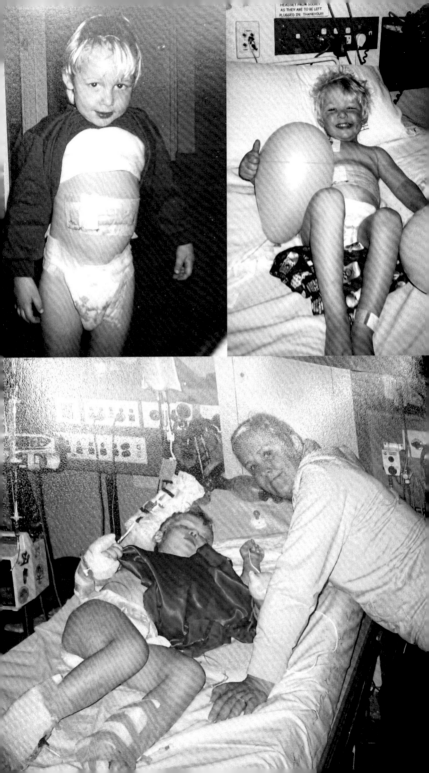

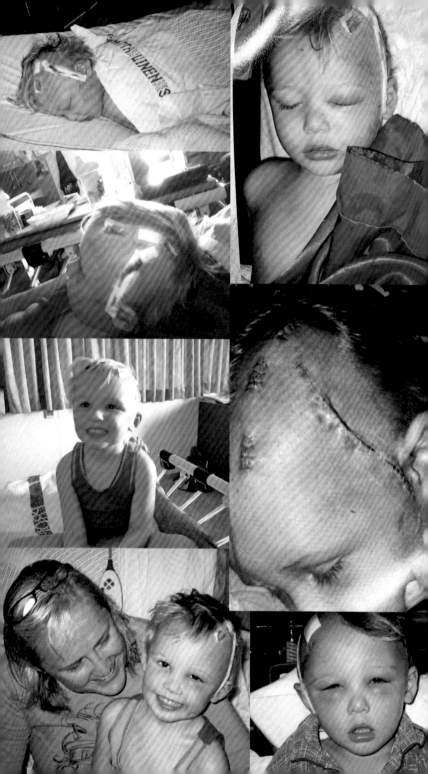

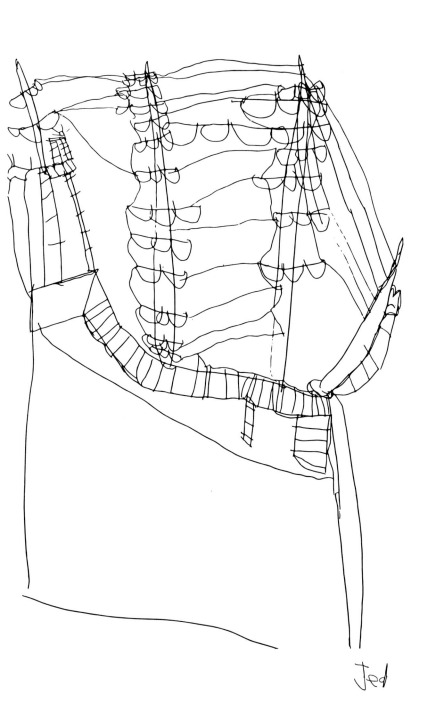

Jed

CHAPTER 19

My Friend Nicole

The first time I met Nicole was when she and I joined a committee called The Torimba Committee, which worked on our town's annual festival. Nicole had a knack for organizing things, and she knew where the party was at. She was tall and blonde at the time, with big blue eyes and something about her just clicked with me.

Her children were the same age as mine, and they all went to the same school. She and I soon became fast friends. We seemed to attract committee work and spent much time together. Nicole was the best distraction and would show up at work anytime. She'd say 'let's order lollies for the fete,' or something similar, which would give me something a whole lot more fun to focus my attention on. She was known to break into my office to redecorate with all manner of sparkles. To this day, I still have filing cabinets full of glitter, and I have kept some of the shiny things that were left behind.

When Jed went for his third brain surgery in October 2012, Nicole and the rest of our Torimba Committee realized that the annual Torimba Ball would be held while we were away with Jed. None of them wanted me to miss out so one evening while in my pyjamas, I was surprised when carloads of women showed up at my doorstep with food, wine, decorations, ball gowns, and a whole lot of glitter. It was simply magical, fun, and so well-planned, I was so grateful. Peter was not impressed the next morning when his toilet seat was covered in glitter, remnants of the night before.

Nicole was an entrepreneur and always looking for something new and interesting to do. She opened a shop in town selling gorgeous ball gowns, bath products, and really nice girly things. Then she moved her attention to making fudge. Her product was called 'Hansel & Gretel's Fudge,' and it was delicious. She took suggestions from her friends about what sort of flavours she should make and it looked like her business was about to boom.

CHAPTER 20

Ravenshoe Café Explosion

When I heard the explosion, I thought it was roadworks. It was loud, and I felt the building shake, but I didn't know what direction the sound came from. I called mum, but she hadn't heard or felt it, so I put it out of my mind.

I received a phone call from a friend, who at the time worked for the local newspaper, and he asked if I was free to go into town for him. He said that he'd heard that someone had driven a car into the back of the cafe, assuming the driver had left their handbrake off. Our town centre was full of sloped roads so cars rolling into the front of shops wasn't really a big deal.

I agreed to take a photograph of the car, and decided it would also be a good excuse to go and see Nicole and grab some lunch while I was out. Work wasn't far from town, but because it was drizzling with rain, I drove my car to the cafe. As I got to the corner of the main street, I noticed heavy black smoke coming from where the explosion had happened and thought to myself, 'this doesn't look good.'

I continued into town and was waved past the café by community members. I could see that the café was on fire and after driving past, did a u-turn, parked, and started to call Nicole, to find out where she was.

When I got to the cafe, I was confronted by the total panic and chaos of everyone around me. There were people everywhere, frantically helping people with their burns. But I couldn't find Nicole. I asked Mellissa, a local off-duty ambulance officer helping apply first-aid to several people if she'd seen Nicole, and she said, "she's in the toilet." All I could think was, 'what toilet?' I spotted another friend helping out and asked her, "where is Nicole?". She replied, "she's in the ablutions, but she's not good."

I raced around to the ablutions, and before I walked in the door, I did a mental check on myself, determined not to let Nicole see the fear on my face. I had done this many times with Jed and knew my calm would transfer to Nicole.

I found Nicole sitting in a white plastic chair, a memory I will never forget.

There was a blonde lady with her, trying to pour water on Nicole, but the tap she was using was a pushbutton tap, and barely gave a trickle of its liquid with each button press. The poor lady was trying her best but had significant difficulties pouring water over my friend. Nicole looked up at me. She had the most gorgeous blue eyes. That was what I focused on.

Nicole's eyes filled with tears as she said "I'm really hurt Nic". I got down on my knees beside her and said, "okay Nic, what do we need to do? Where does it hurt the most? What do you need?"

As I looked down, I realized my hands were shaking. I consciously tried to stop that from happening in front of her. I told her that I was going to call her husband, and she said that she was going to pass out. I said, "that's okay, honey. I'll go and get some help." I got up and left Nicole with the blond lady, who was still pouring water over Nicole's burns. As I ran out of the ablutions block, I collided with Annie, Nicole's sister-in-law. She had been searching for Nicole. I said, "she's in there," and ushered her towards the ablutions block.

I ran to find Darryl, an ambulance officer, whom I grabbed and told that Nicole was in a bad way and needed to be seen straight away. He and I ran back into the ablutions block, found a blanket, and put it on the grass for Nicole. Darryl said that sitting in a chair was not good for Nicole, so we all helped to move her to the blanket outside. By this time, we had wrapped her the best we could in glad wrap in an effort to retain heat. I held Nicole's hands the whole way out of the ablutions block, while she was lying down outside and for the rest of the time, I was with her that day. She had incredibly long dainty fingers.

Nicole told us that she was having trouble breathing. We called for the local General Practitioner, Dr. Connolly, who gave her an injection of pain relief. He recommended that she be put in an ambulance as soon as possible. I don't know how long we sat there in the rain with Nicole. I could hear my phone ringing in my pocket, but I couldn't answer it; I was too focused on Nicole, holding her hands and talking to her. I found out later that it was Peter trying to call me, who was sick with worry about my whereabouts after the explosion. Neither of us realized that we were a matter of metres away from each other, but he couldn't find me due to the absolute war zone between us.

I continued holding onto Nicole's hands as a team helped lift Nicole onto a stretcher. Faces from that day have been etched into my memory; we are all haunted. There was Terry, who helped lift Nicole, and stood ashen-faced and helpless. Kim and Jayme stood outside the ambulance, waiting and standing in vigil. Nicole's husband, Shane, and Chris soon arrived.

Nicole was declining rapidly, so was pulled out of the ambulance to receive urgent medical attention, which included I.V. fluids. A circle of love surrounded her as we held blankets to protect her privacy (people were trying to take photos of her). The ambulance officers told me very clearly that I needed to tell Nicole how much I loved her. Time went on, but it seemed to stand still as we stood in the middle of the road with Nicole that day.

A medevac helicopter had been called to transport Nicole to Townsville hospital. As her ambulance slowly made its way to the helicopter landing pad, I realized that my whole body felt tense and rigid, frozen by all the drama. I had told Nicole how much I loved her, and there was nothing more I could do.

I walked slowly back to my car without stopping to help anyone else. I needed to rest. I saw a few friends, and they asked me how Nicole was, and that's when I lost it. I lost all control as I walked up the street, knowing that my emotions must have been shocking to some of the people I saw. I called Peter and asked him to pick up the children from school. I drove to my mum's home, knowing it was the closest place where there was somebody for me.

When I got to my mum's house, I turned on the TV to realize that the coverage of the explosion was substantial. I began ringing my and Peter's family to let them know we were all ok, but they would probably see me amidst the chaos on the TV. I then let my Facebook contacts know that the Bakers were all ok.

In the coming days, I filled myself with manifestations that Nicole would be fine and would need her tribe to help her recover from her injuries. I called her sister-in-law to let her know that the local church was praying for Nicole, but I could sense from the tone of her voice that something wasn't right. She said that Shane had been told it was time to 'turn off the machines' as Nicole's injuries were too severe to survive. I hung up the phone and collapsed. Mum comforted me, understanding the gravity of the situation. She, too, fell to the floor and lay on top of me, holding me as tight as she could, and there we stayed until I was spent.

It's very hard to describe the remainder of that week and the coming weeks. Nicole was constantly on my mind, willing her to hold on, fight, and survive. The media were suddenly everywhere in our small town.

My conversations with Nicole didn't stop, nor did with Billie, Nicole's parents and daughter. They had been on a European cruise, desperately trying to get home to see Nicole. Billie was the travel agent who booked the cruise, and her message to me was to ask if the explosion was at Hans and Vicki's café. Billie went above and beyond to try every avenue to bring them home to be with Nicole. When they landed in Australia, they were ferried to the hospital. I was with them emotionally the whole time.

Peter had gone away for the night on school camp with Jed because we agreed that we needed to try and keep things as normal as possible for the kids' sake. I was alone with two sleeping children on the night they returned, I couldn't sleep because I knew that these were the final hours for Nicole. I talked to her, and I told her how proud I was of her and how strong she had been to fight for as long as she had. I called her very bad names because that's what we did on the phone, and I told her that mum and dad were nearly there. Sometime in the early morning, I received a message that Nicole is now with the angels.

CHAPTER 21

Recovery

The explosion was a pivotal point in my life. I tried the best I could to help the community when asked. I was doing everything I could. However, the scars run deep when you go through an experience like this.

When Nicole died, I was repeatedly referred to in the media as her best friend, when in fact, she had Kim, and I had my Kym, two beautiful best friends to the two 'Nics.' Little did the media realize that small detail caused substantial emotional distress and added to the weight and grief of the situation.

I don't think that I was able to come to terms with the explosion until after the findings of the Coroner were released. Speaking to the Coroner directly helped me reconcile the shocking loss of my friend Nicole.

Before her death, Nicole had been encouraging me to go and see a Clairvoyant to seek insight into Jed's future. Sadly, I never got to go with Nicole, but six months after the explosion, I felt ready to give in to my curiosity and hopefully connect with Nicole.

A confessed skeptic, I had Mum use a false name when booking to see the 'Secretary', as she liked to be called. My identity as Nicole's 'best friend' was well-known by that time due to the national coverage of the explosion. I had become used to seeing my face and name in the media, including in newspapers and on a current affairs TV show, 60 Minutes. I didn't want my loss of anonymity to impact my experience with the Secretary.

Two days after Christmas in 2015, I sat in a chair while the Secretary 'dialed in.' I found her incredibly kind and ethereal on meeting, which allowed my trust and emotions to build.

As she began, the Secretary described a very strong female personality wanting to connect with me. She described her as having blue hair and wearing pink. She had a leprechaun with her and laughed as she bounced a ball. The candle in the room was what kept her attention the most. It was very clear to me that it was Nicole connecting with me that day, and I left feeling uplifted by messages of love and healing.

From then on, I continued to meet with Nicole via the Secretary, and I quickly realized that even though Nicole was no longer alive, she was still with me and had very big plans. With her guidance, I started my own charity (Moyamoya Australia), where I have achieved many goals, held certain events, and led me to my purpose.

●

CHAPTER 22

Joseph, The Comet

My sister Mandy is a strong woman who has lived remotely in Australia and Papua New Guinea. She has been a farmer's wife and stayed home with her three children while her husband worked away. Early on, we had a fairly rocky relationship, but after the explosion and the breakdown of her marriage, we became very close.

All three of Mandy's kids have become close companions to their cousins, my children. Kelsie loves music and netball, Joseph a fishing and AFL fanatic, and Erin, the youngest of the family, is a real empath.

Joseph's love of footy started very early. He trained hard, he played hard, and he was good. So good, in fact, that Joseph was selected as an Academy Player for the Gold Coast Suns AFL team. We all anticipated that Joseph would be an AFL superstar, either as a player or an Executive. He was known as 'Joey' to his mates and 'Jos' to his mum.

When Joseph was 16 years old, he took a knock to the head during a footy game and was taken to the hospital for a precautionary head scan. I remember receiving the phone call from Mandy that day, saying that the scan had revealed a mass on Joseph's upper cheekbone, believed to be a tumour. Further tests concluded that Joseph had a rare, aggressive cancer called Rhabdomyosarcoma.

My sister and her boy were then forced onto the treadmill of chronic illness, living away from home so Joseph could receive treatment. Mandy calmly managed this stage of Joseph's journey with class and composure, rarely showing a wrinkle in her demeanour.

While Joseph received treatment in Brisbane with Mandy by his side, Erin lived abroad on a student exchange, and Kelsie lived in Melbourne, also as a student. Once they both returned home, they visited their brother often and witnessed his fight for life.

Just before Christmas in 2020, a scan of Joseph's brain revealed sudden and substantial shrinkage of the tumour. It meant an extended period of time at home over Christmas for Joseph and Mandy, which was a blessing for us all.

Sadly in the new year, Joseph's health began to decline as the tumour decided to raise its ugly head again. The thing about Rhabdomyosarcoma is that it is aggressive. Joseph and Mandy returned to Brisbane for ongoing treatment as he bravely fought for his life once again. In April of 2021, he was able to attend Kelsie's 21st birthday in Melbourne, which would be their final family celebration with Joseph. On 13th June 2021, Joseph, the warrior, the bright light, my comet, and one of the most incredible humans I have been blessed to know, lost his fight with cancer.

Joseph was celebrated at the biggest sporting stadium in Cairns, packed to the rafters with everyone he loved, and saluted off the field with a guard of honour. I walked behind my sister as Joseph made his final journey out of the stadium. It was a surreal experience that was hard to accept. It was not supposed to be Joseph that lost his fight. I had been very aware of Jed's mortality for many years, and it felt like the universe had taken the wrong boy.

On reflection, I realize that it's really shitty odds for two sisters to both share a rare diagnosis for their children. Mums like us are often recipients of frustrating statements like, "I don't know how you do it," or, "I wouldn't cope," but the reality is, we don't have a choice. If we had a choice, our families wouldn't spend their lives watching children fight against life-threatening illnesses.

Joseph's passing made the front page of the Cairns Post, and the story was carried nationally. It was such a profound loss for the AFL community in Cairns and the whole of AFL Australia.

I call Joseph my comet because he was so bright, fast, and went very quickly, as opposed to the slow burn that is Jed. To this day, I struggle to reconcile Joseph's loss. I simply don't understand it. #FuckCancer

CHAPTER 23

The Thing About Jed

I feel that my experiences with trauma, love, and loss have changed me for the better.

It took me a long time to recover from the explosion, but when Nicole was losing her life in front of me, I could draw from my experiences with Jed to show her calm, not panic. I believe that in the last moments of her consciousness, I could carry the burden of fear and guide her peacefully into her soul's final moments on earth. I could tell her how much I loved her when so many loved ones don't get that opportunity. Nicole had a team of cheerleaders with her that day, and I genuinely feel blessed that I was one of them.

The thing about Jed is all in the perception. I understand that people see me struggle with him; his disability can be overwhelming. He has the body of a man and the testosterone of a teenager but a child's reasoning ability.

Recently, Jed and I were away from home for medical appointments, so we checked into a hotel for the night. Check-in was at the hotel's bar, so we were standing close to a group of men who were drinking. I could hear the men flippantly swearing as they conversed with each other and stood nervously, as swearing was something that Jed didn't respond well to. Jed shot the men a look that resulted in one of the older men aggressively bellowing, "what are you looking at?" Unfortunately for the fellow, Jed's disability wasn't visible, so he was shocked when I turned around and clapped back, "this is what a childhood stroke looks like."

Later that evening, Jed and I returned to the bar for a beer for me and apple juice for Jed. The man from earlier must have realized that he was too quick to judge, and all credit to him approached us and apologized. I had already decided that I was going to approach him, but he made the situation easier for me. We had a conversation that ended with a hug and forgiveness.

This is what I have learned from Jed. I believe he was sent to me to give me purpose and show the world how awesome he is, regardless of his diagnosis. To showcase how someone with a considerable disability can teach anyone in the mainstream how to be a good human. He has consistently brought people together and taught us how to be better.

Jed has helped me recognize my strengths and weaknesses and where my energy should be spent.

These days, I make better choices and distance myself from those with negative energy, surrounding myself with people who take a higher pathway and find the silver lining in every situation. I will admit that some days are harder than others, and the ups and downs continue. Peter sees me at my worst, finding me rocking in a corner, crying, frustrated, and hurt. The record player in my head is my worst enemy, so I get help when needed. My mental health was a focus for me when I went through the worst with Jed, but my fragility was tested again with Nicole's death and Joseph's loss. Sometimes, I still struggle. There are, understandably, days when I need to disconnect from everything, put on a headset, and do a jigsaw puzzle.

I allow myself time for healing, and on bad days I sit with my grief and let it wash over me. I also get up the next day, acknowledging that the day before had been awful but that today was a new day. Just get up and keep going. This is another skill I have learned from Jed.

Learning from him daily is the thing about Jed.

ACKNOWLEDGEMENTS

This story would never have been told had it not been for the love and support of so many mentioned in this book.

Firstly, we had some wonderful support from the Baker family. Grandma Norma, Sue, Trish, Janet, and Isabella in Brisbane, for your visits and support, for taking us away from the hospital and making us sit in the park with our backs to the building so we couldn't see the hospital. That quiet time away from the battle zone was extremely sustaining. Vanessa, your skills at taking that blood pressure when we needed it most, and for trekking across Sydney to see us, and Jenni and Gav for visiting us in the hospital. We thank you for all of the messages and love from you all.

The Chapmans, Kym, my bestie, in hospital with us on more than one occasion, holding it together when Captain Starlight was singing *Twinkle Twinkle Little Star* to Jed and holding my hand when I wasn't able to keep it together. For knowing exactly what we needed and when we needed it. Chantal and Jon, for your care, while we were in Sydney and our home away from home.

The Ramsay's, you seriously don't know how good for my soul you are. Sean has seen me at my worst, usually very early in the morning, with crazy hair; you have always gone out of your way to provide strength to Jed and me. Simone, your visits were uplifting and so gratefully received, and Jackie, you were a piece of my mum when I needed it.

Those who had a hand in changing Jed's room. The surprise on that day lifted our spirits and set us up just right for recovery.

Dr. Tim Warnock, who has now become like family to us. Without your dedication to our plight, we may never have been able to keep Jed for so long; thank you.

To the Team at Sydney Children's Hospital, Dr. Ian Andrews, Dr. Andrew Rosenberg, and Dr. Fiona Mackie, you are leading examples of how holistic medical management of a complex and chronic case should be managed. We are forever in your debt.

Professor Marcus Stoodley, I have joked that you are God over the years. You really are. You have saved Jed, and you have saved me on so many levels. Your calm in the storm was the most comforting experience, and we simply cannot express the gratitude we, and all of your other Moyamoya patients, feel toward you.

Bree, for once, I had a dream.

The All American Car Club of Cairns has been in our corner since before Jed was born. They are extended family to us, and their love and support over the years have been unwavering.

SYNT. You know who you are, and the cookies were so fine.

To our fellow Moyamoya Warriors, those we still have, those we have lost along the way. Your journeys have been important to us all. Your strength is our strength. Your courage is the stuff of legends, and we are so happy to have formed our community.

To all of the supporters of Moyamoya Australia. From the very first day we started on this journey, never in our wildest dreams did we imagine that it would go as far as it is going and will continue to grow. Every raffle ticket, every share of our social media, every single conversation, thank you.

My Moyamoya Australia All Stars, you signed up, and you showed up for me, and we have lifelong friendships and memories from that experience. Thank you.

To every business that has sponsored us for our fundraising, events, and prizes.

The Ravenshoe Community. They say it takes a village to raise a child, and this is more apparent when you are living with a difficult and unpredictable disease, and the township has embraced us and kept us afloat since the day we first moved here.

To my Mum for keeping the Home Fires burning and my Dad for getting dirty on the battlefield with me.

Peter, Charlie, Lucy, I am no one without you. I can't even begin to articulate what you are to me; you are the most incredible family, I love you; you are my world.

And to Jed, who has the inspiration for change, my Master, my Captain, thank you for choosing me.

Working with Nicola on the publication of "The Thing About Jed" has been an incredible honour. During my first read-through of the manuscript, I realized that Nicola had captured the essence of what it meant to be a survivor. Her harrowing experience with her son's diagnosis, an untimely explosion, and one powerful friendship created her truly inspiring story.

I wish Nicola all the success and happiness in her new endeavour as a published author. I have no doubt that "The Thing About Jed" will touch the hearts of many around the world.

Crystal Leonardi
Bowerbird Publishing
www.crystalleonardi.com